AF426671

Published by
Mind's Eye Publications™
985 Deborah Avenue
Elgin, IL 60123-1918
mindseyepublications.com

Cover Art by Dan Sauer

The Nothing Box
& Other Poems

The Nothing Box

& Other Poems

By Steven Withrow

Author's Note

My goal for this book was straightforward: to collect 50 of my best
dark poems before my 50th birthday in March 2024.

Such a small book from a prose writer might be considered a trifle,
a single novella or a slim sheaf of short stories. For a poet,
however, this is a gigantic undertaking, if the aim is to ensure each
poem rewards a reader's close attention. It can take a lifetime,
and early drafts of a few poems here date back 30 years.

Many of the poems have appeared in my previous chapbooks and in
various publications (see the acknowledgments page at the back of
the book), but several are new to this collection. The title poem pays
homage to *A Box of Nothing*, a 1985 children's novel by the late
English author and poet Peter Dickinson (1927-2015), which I read
when I was 11.

A note about genre: I do not write horror. I don't write to flat-out ter-
rify or to prompt revulsion, though I'm not opposed to doing so at se-
lect moments. Horror can emerge from any genre, and poems in this
collection encompass cautionary science fiction, classic ghost stories,
and dark fantasy in the modes of Ray Bradbury and Shirley Jackson.

Verse is meant to be said and heard as well as read, so I'll also
be making audio recordings available online.

Now it's time to open the box and to see what isn't there.

Contents

I

Caged Animals

Caged Animals

The girl I was was a timid mouse
When we came to stay at the summer house
  Of Crazy Jane, my mother's friend.
  (She earned that nickname, in the end.)
She had no children, nor a spouse;

She seemed to be from a grander age
Of passenger ships, or the opera stage;
  Wore dressing gowns and her hair pinned up;
  She served me tea in a china cup;
And she kept a cockatoo in a cage.

The white-bodied bird had a yellow crest,
A curved black bill. And as a guest,
  Though shy of Jane, I could approach
  That imposing cage and quietly coach
Him to mimic a phrase: *You love me best.*

I fed him grapes as we worked on words;
He wasn't among the most brilliant birds,
  But we practiced for hours. Then Jane swept in
  While Mom was resting: "You won't be kin
To creatures till you've joined their herds

Or flocks; have dwelt in the fox's den
Or the honeybee's box." And when
  I tried to ask her how she knew
  So much about the cockatoo,
She signed the air, in feather pen,

And thus transformed me. Here I perch,
The white bird's mate. I've ceased my search
  For methods of escape. She turned
  Mom to a toad, and I have learned
To be stone, like a gargoyle on a church.

Jane visits us less frequently,
But she adds to her menagerie
  Each time she does. There's now a crow
  Who used to be a man, and a doe
With a woman's eyes. And I can see

My mate was once a human boy.
We cannot speak, but still enjoy
  The silences. (Mom died last year.)
  Strangely, there's an egg, I fear,
To save from Jane, I must destroy.

Ghosts in Their Sunday Clothes

Ghosts in their Sunday clothes are leaving town
As more arrive in homespun every week.
The dress of death is always trending down.

The woman in white, of late, is wearing brown;
The suicide's ensemble's now antique.
Ghosts in their Sunday clothes are leaving town.

The long-dead heiress sells her sleekest gown
To a legless phantom void of all mystique.
The dress of death is always trending down.

Even the graveyard king, who found his crown
When he lost his head, is fleeing with the chic.
Ghosts in their Sunday clothes are leaving town,

And their keening's nearly loud enough to drown
The low hiss of the living, so to speak.
The dress of death is always trending down.

Though fashion snobs might meet it with a frown,
The local situation's not unique:
Yes, ghosts in their Sunday clothes are leaving town,
But the dress of death is *always* trending down.

The Scourge of Song

Bedbugs had brought the Scourge of Song
  To our quaint suburban town of Weems,
And when we first saw something wrong—
  Our children woke from violent dreams
  Singing what we thought were themes
From operas—we called their shrinks,
  Who upped their meds. But now it seems
We should have sought the Theban Sphinx.

Our sons and daughters chanted puzzles
  That no one older could unriddle.
A few considered fitting muzzles
  Over their moving mouths. One brittle
  Father needing sleep did fiddle
With a cocktail of numbing drinks,
  But most of us, we trod the middle.
We should have sought the Theban Sphinx.

The coded songs were in a tongue
  That might have been Sumerian
For all we followed what they'd sung.
  Our toddlers, like Assyrian
  Seers—*hardly Presbyterian*—
Interrupted our forty winks.
  We tried to act Shakespearean
But should have sought the Theban Sphinx.

A week's gone by; the Scourge has spread
  To orioles and bobolinks.
The birdsong blots the air with dread.
  We should have sought the Theban Sphinx.

Designer Ghosts

To make my living I'm designing ghosts.
Those confined to churchyard haunts are flawed;
My phantoms mingle better with their hosts.
I earn my paycheck—*face it*—playing God.
The wraiths and shades of old were no doubt apt
For sensibilities convinced that souls
Persist in spectral energies untapped
By mortals, though the theory's full of holes.
New Metaphysics tells us rattled brains
Spin spirits out, as a spider does a thread.
My oeuvre has a hundred novel strains,
But there's no strong connection with the dead.
How queer, then, I should generate a ghoul
That shrieks as my late father did—*the fool.*

The Druggist's Curse

The druggist had been married twice. And once
He'd finalized his second divorce and paid
The settlement, he moved from Mapleshade
(To stay in town, he'd have to be a dunce)
Back east to Albany, where he's lived since.
Estranged from family and having never made
Too many friends outside the cavalcade
Of hangers-on his two wives could convince
To stick around, the druggist went to work
At a hospital pharmacy on the graveyard shift.
He stopped himself from flirting with the nurses
When he struck out with one and got a smirk
Of—*was it pity?*—in response. To lift
His nights from malaise, he chose to study curses.

The druggist's research led him to a site
Called "Mostly Modern Potions & New Hexes"
From a witchy type known merely as Alexis.
He read through it by day then worked by night
(Adopting a vampiric scorn of light)
And when he slept he dreamed of both his exes,
Engaged with them in battles of the sexes
Involving guns and axes. More than spite
Compelled the druggist to purloin what parts
He needed from locked shelves to mix a draft
Of a tasteless, odorless poison he named "Brink."
At a bar for drunks and sad Miss Lonelyhearts
He chatted up a girl, and when she laughed
He tipped his hidden dram into her drink.

What Came of the Search

In the catastrophic neighborhoods of Gorham,
    In the rubble of the Saturnine assault,
Where, day sixteen, the searchers from the Forum,
Having found no souls or bodies, called a halt,
    A startled spotter, scraping half a mouse
        From cellar ashes, said,
        Expecting only dead:
There is someone else alive in this old house.

On a wireless set twelve miles away in Hodd
    A uniformed communicant relayed
This message to Sir Favored-More-By-God,
And up the chain of favorites, grade by grade,
    Went word of what the spotter had made clear
        In chatter above his caste
        (Which may have been his last):
The tetrapods left someone living here.

As a consequence of finding the survivor
    The wearied searchers, lessened in their shame,
Were told their quarry was a sand-truck driver
But were not grand enough to learn her name,
    So, when their children asked them for the story
        Of how they fared in Hell,
        They merely could retell:
The lady had no face, and drove a lorry.

The Bedlam Philharmonic

Hank hates these concerts, finds them cloying,
But Lisa loves them, so here they are
On the mezzanine. Below, the star
Conductor preens. What's more annoying,
He turned down Red Sox tickets to make
His woman happy. *For heaven's sake,*

Let's wrap this up already, he thinks.
This Mahler song's ten hours long.
Just then he sees there's something wrong
With the lady playing cello. He blinks
And looks again. She sways in her chair,
With bony fingers, snaky hair.

The other players haven't changed,
Il Maestro hasn't missed a beat,
And Lisa's frozen to her seat
Oblivious to how deranged
The demon cellist now appears,
A fusion of his inmost fears.

Hank splutters, points, and nearly stands,
And Lisa briskly clears her throat
To show she's hanging on every note.
Woodwinds wheeze. The harpy's hands,
Outsized like crab claws, strangle strings,
And at her back, black angel's wings.

Mahler ends; crowd applauds;
Star conductor soaks it in;
Cellist gives a shark-toothed grin
As if to say that fiendish gods
Had favored theirs of all domains
With dismal and abysmal strains

Of noise, though Hank alone receives
The twisted signal. A standing ovation
Reverses the freakish transformation
In the cellist's frame. His brain believes
Such alteration's bunk. His eyes,
However, tell him otherwise.

At intermission, leaving the hall,
Lisa scowls, mistaking shock
For scorn on Hank's face, white as chalk.
"Next time stay home and watch baseball,"
She sneers and waits for Hank's dumb joke,
But none comes. It's like he's had a stroke

Or grand mal seizure. Choking, he stumbles
Against the wall and drops to the floor,
And Lisa's by his side and yelling for
Someone to call a doctor. He mumbles.
His fevered head is in her lap,
His round mouth closing like a trap.

The Interlopers

They entered through my mirror.
I watched them, once, last year
Take shape and test the glass
On the other side. To pass
Themselves from there to here
Was an act of force. The clearer
They appeared to me, the less
I looked the stunned admirer
Who'd gone to comb my hair
And ended up aware
(Who made me the inquirer?)
Of the interlopers. I guess
That name fits what they are.
Their arrival led to a loss
Of speech, and a blinding terror
I still can't shake. My error,
As I saw them press the gloss,
Was to misconceive how far
They'd come in coming nearer.
(Had I given them, through fear,
A door?) They moved en masse,
But massless, like a gas
Unloosed in war. *Our dear*,
They said, crashing my mirror.

Second Sight

Logging trucks avoid the road
Where the river meets the ridge.
Years ago, one tipped its load
Veering on a narrow bridge
When a wounded eagle showed
Bloodied feathers, tattered tail,
Landing on a lamp-lit rail.

Why the driver lost control
(He told his rescuers he'd seen,
Lifting from the bird, a soul,
Like a ghost from a machine)
Is still uncertain. As a whole,
Loggers, though their path is slowed,
Choose to ride a longer road.

The Nothing Box

By rights, I should have left the box alone:
Round and white, perfect for a trilby hat
Or a small cake. I pushed aside the cat
Pawing it on the bed, and had I known
What agonies it held or how it got
Consigned to me from nowhere, I would not
Have touched it, but the error was my own
In any case—I'd *wanted* to look inside.
And so I bent and saw that it was tied
With finely knotted string, which I undid.
Then, lifting off the fancy cardboard lid,
I goggled down at blackest emptiness
Like a sunspot pressed to fit within a sack.
Whoever sent the box gave no address,
Assured that I could never send it back.

II

The Cruel Become Werewolves

The Cruel Become Werewolves

The cruel contract lycanthropy and grow
More visibly hirsute. The moon is not
Involved, unless a charge of lunacy
Is warranted, and some say this is so,
But no one's offered evidential proof,
And God knows if it's cursed or if it's caught.

To illustrate the change, we'll cite the case
Of Morris Incaviglia, salesman for
Amalgamated Sundries Limited,
Who drove a yellow Saab from place to place
And would seek out, when circumstance allowed,
A pass-through town without a country store

For many miles, and then he'd settle on
That town's most precious landmark; it could be
A covered bridge now closed to cars, a church
The founders built, its first bell tower gone
In some great winter storm, but still a gem,
Or even just an ivy-tangled tree

At the town's lone four-way stop. And finding it,
The salesman would return at night to toss
A Mason jar of flaming kerosene
Straight at its most incendiary bit.
He'd often lob a second or a third,
Ensuring it would be a total loss.

Then Morris, groomed impeccably, would drive
Until the razored stubble on his cheeks
Became a scraggly beard. His canine teeth
Would lengthen, too. But he felt no more alive,
And with less wolfish strength, than when he burned.
We estimate he'd had the plague for weeks.

Glenwell's Son

In Albert's mind, the uninvited one
At each work fête was Glenwell's murdered son.
The dead boy came to office feasts—he haunted
The August sales retreat, a thing unwanted—
But Glenwell had his name above the door,
So younger staffers gasped and said no more.

The year the dead boy's body met the worm
Was the first of Albert's tenure with the firm.
A drifter had surrendered and confessed;
Still, Glenwell's son seemed disinclined to rest.
Now, at the Christmas singalong, each note
Sticks like a thumb in Albert's guilty throat.

A Blue Giraffe

Tim's wife collected figurines
Of animals in colored glass.
Their house had shelves of blues and greens—
Her favorite shades—and when he'd pass
An artists' fair or antiques shop
On business trips, he'd sometimes stop
To add to her menagerie.
Tim loved his wife, and though away
As often as twice a month, he'd stay
At home with her when he was free.

While walking once in Boston, Tim
Had stumbled on what seemed to him
To be a gypsy's ancient carriage.
On second glance, it was just a cart,
And the seller said, "*I know your heart.
Childless, but a pleasant marriage
With few regrets.*" Tim stood there staring.
This tall young woman read him well.
He wondered if the suit he was wearing
Or else his face had been the tell.

In his pocket, a phone buzzed. He paused
To check the caller, and the number
He knew but had not expected to see.
It had been weeks. He'd told Marie
She shouldn't get in touch. They'd caused
Enough of a stir, he thought, in the wake
Of their rendezvous in May. He'd dropped
The ball in trying to disencumber
Himself of the bulk of that mistake.
He waited till the buzzing stopped.

The seller had a row of boxes
On a tabletop display. She tapped
On one; its paper came unwrapped;
Its lid slid back; a pair of foxes,
Red and gold, jumped tinkling out
And scampered, crystalline, about
The tiny stage. Tim, dumbstruck, gaped.
The seller did some sleight-of-hand,
And from a bigger box escaped
A yellow ostrich with a purple band

Around its tail. The clumsy bird,
With cartoon swiftness, danced a jig,
Which woke an orange bear (absurd
As it was to see) and a silver pig
That almost shattered in its race
To the table's edge, but the seller swooped
Like a hungry buzzard, low, and scooped
The errant beast into its case.
She then revealed—Tim had to laugh—
The perfect gift: *a blue giraffe.*

He paid a pittance for the piece,
But the seller balked when he offered more.
"There's not its like in any store,"
She said instead. "Your wife, Elise,
Will treasure this. She favors blue."
And Tim admitted this was true.
He'd given up on playing sleuth,
Ignoring how she'd guessed the truth.
"*A warning, though,*" she called him back,
"*Your heart will falter should this crack.*"

Tim treated the package with too much care
For its price and worth. But he had to allow
That peddler woman left him rattled:
Her street-fair psychic's tricks, the scare
She'd put in him. *And who knew how
Those goddamn glass things sprang to life
Before his eyes?* He felt embattled
By vengeful forces. The box of doom
He locked in a safe in his hotel room
Until he could go back to his wife.

Flying home, Tim cradled the gem
Like an egg, a tulip on a stem.
It could not move to raise its head,
This blue giraffe Elise would cherish.
Then turbulence shook up the plane.
(He knew he should have caught a train.)
The glass form tumbled from his grip,
And striking the floor broke off a chip
Of blue....
          No cause for Tim to perish;
A nurse in coach pronounced him dead.

Scabrous Oak
(*Quercus scabrosus*)

Lightning has blasted any number
of other oaks, and drought has thinned
a line of hemlocks, useless lumber
lost to the mill or the killing wind—

yet *this* is not a blighted tree
infested, root to crown, with weevils,
but a totem of indecency
and stranger, more invasive evils.

An arborist, with different words
for the same plant without the need
to moralize, observes a bird's
approach but does not intercede

when, like a whip, a limb goes slack
and then flicks up to catch the prize
a knocking blow and a twiggy thwack
that boggle human ears and eyes.

Such motion, in a wizard's book,
might almost be explained away
by giving it a second look
through a magic lens. But who can say

what happens to the battered wren
after it hits the trunk? Do trees
grow scabrous lips and teeth like men?
There is no name for this disease.

The Flower-Faced Boy At The Mall

It's fine to stare. The boy's become inured
To fixed expressions of unease. It's fine
As well to whisper a note of pity. At nine,
Or as young as six, he's already endured
Both shame and sympathy. Be reassured:
The nature of his plight is by design,
Though why Creation took this freakish line
Is hard to see. His face cannot be cured.

Which flower he most resembles is the game.
The food court ladies hold that he's a rose;
His forehead buds are pink, his yellow cheeks
Puff out like pansies. No one has a name
For the vegetal assemblage of his nose.
The boy could tell us, but he never speaks.

The Gray Kid

I

The Gray kid called the teen addiction line
And got a veteran volunteer named Pine
Who'd manned the phone two evening shifts a week
Since his husband died. The kids who called were not
So desperate yet they needed meds; he thought
They mostly wanted someone who wouldn't freak
And didn't always stick to script. Past nine,
The Gray kid called to say he'd used Divine.

He said his name was "Gray," or maybe "Grey."
He said the tablet was a pale pink dot
But didn't say who sold it. "I was weak,"
He said. His voice went soft when he started to speak
And quickly rose with a boyish creak. "I fought
Divine at first, then I let it have its way."

II

The hotline's training course taught Pine to mark
Those callers who'd tried D. Not to narc
Them out and turn them in, but rather to
Count users of the scariest street fix
For public health. Two hundred dead, and six
ODs in town that month alone. Pine knew
The myths: that D will make you see in the dark
Or boost your strength, and many another lark.

But Gray's account was different. "All I felt
Was agony, which then began to mix
With a soothing sense of stillness. I could do
Nothing but stand there as a hole poked through
My bedroom wall. A sound like breaking sticks.
And God emerged, so fierce and bright I knelt."

III

At that point Pine had heard enough and asked
If Gray was using D right now, as tasked
By the hotline script. The kid got quiet then;
His purple prose went black. A minute passed,
And Pine thought he'd clicked off, but at the last
Moment before Pine checked, Gray spoke again:
"God holds me in His light. In Him I've basked.
He's present here with me, His face unmasked."

Worried now that Gray was more than high,
Pine pressed him to dial 911. In the past,
This simple urging worked with kids, but when
Gray shouted out, Pine flinched and dropped his pen.
"I can't get free! No! Help me! I——" A blast
Of static, then a hush. A strangled cry.

IV

Nightmares of space—the starry vacuum—came,
And once Pine learned to shut them out, their claim
On his mind redoubled, adding monstrous forms,
Peculiar constellations, to the void:
Symbols linking Kierkegaard and Freud,
A gaping eye the red of Martian storms,
Four hands juggling blistered balls of flame,
And wormlike uglies Pine could never name.

Pine didn't quit the hotline, but he skipped
Three shifts before he felt less paranoid
And able to resume his daily norms.
Recalling Gray, he saw black flies in swarms,
So he kept himself, by force of will, employed
With secret grieving, cleaving to the script.

Rats

The rats, as one, dismiss our proferred terms:
Stay deep beneath the streets, or die by gas.
For centuries we feared them for their germs,
But rats these days are of a higher class.
And now our public panic has its source
In cognitive increase. Like a race horse
Restructured to run ninety miles an hour,
A rat's small brain has twice the mental power

Of a chimp's brain. (That ratio is flawed,
And chimp is to rat as human is to god,
New studies show us.) How they broke their cages,
And circumvented lockdown protocols
To flee the lab, is a question for the ages.
They've settled in our churches, shopping malls,
And gleaming glass-and-metal office blocks.
They've hacked the grid and, so far, shun peace talks.

We're armed with bioweapons strong enough
To bomb them from the gene pool should our bluff
Be called. We'd rather, though, preserve our gains
And keep intact the wetware of their brains.
The rats, we think, will parley to survive
Come winter when we freeze and starve them out;
Persistence is an urgent mammal drive.
They're eager to capitulate, no doubt.

When Mother Taught Me Hymns

When Mother taught me hymns, she'd hum
And pound our old harmonium.
I'd sing along, a Christian child,
"Gentle Jesus, meek and mild,"

But later, when I'd sing alone,
The Devil's brutal baritone
Convulsed in me, deranged each chord:
"Thou hast forsaken me, O Lord."

When Mother taught me hymns, she'd cry
With credence in her voice, and I
Cried too, in chorus with her spirit,
So loudly all the town could hear it,

But later, when I'd learned control,
And wouldn't pray to save my soul,
I waited for the Beast to come
And played that black harmonium.

The Green-Eyed Man

There was no call for epilogue.
    The telling of her soul
Was like a Marple mystery;
    Her story ended whole.

For prologue, too, the need was nil.
    Her family bore no shame.
About her birthplace news was scarce,
    No scandal to its name.

Her parents ran a jewelry store.
    When they retired to Vale,
She, nearing thirty, shuttered it
    And put it up for sale.

The profits netted were enough
    To sign a one-year lease
On a modest coastal studio
    Where she could paint in peace.

She walked the beach each morning and
    She tried to sketch the sea,
To catch the wheeling flight of gulls,
    But for some reason she

Could only draw a single face:
    A man she did not know.
When friends stopped by, they wondered if
    She had a secret beau.

She'd been in love, but sadly so.
    It had gone unrequited.
Hard seasons pining for her teacher
    Bruised, her spirit blighted.

The green-eyed man looked nothing like
    Her Dutch design instructor,
And she was glad to leave the daze
    From which harsh time had plucked her.

Weeks on, her walls were papered with
    His face, his strange green eyes.
In pencil, ink, and chalk pastels
    She held him like a prize.

Two months of this, and visitors
    Grew worried she was ill.
And one said make a break from art.
    And one said take a pill.

One night she tore her pictures down
    And burned them in a barrel.
She half-expected Marley's ghost
    To flee *A Christmas Carol*

And waft up with the pulpy smoke
    To warn her of her fate.
She thought she might be going mad.
    She feared it was too late.

A year, and she still never found
    A memory or trace
Of the presence of the green-eyed man.
    She'd almost blocked his face.

Her lease expired. She moved to town.
    She left her paints behind.
She got a part-time job; at least
    She hadn't lost her mind.

Yet walking home she swore she saw
    That man, as through a fog.
A closer look showed someone else.
    This was no epilogue.

(What climax could she claim for a life
    That, like a shoddy scape,
Lacked composition, skewed perspective—
    A wreck of color, shape?)

At home, the hallway mirror caught
    Her face. *Her eyes were green,*
Beneath a kind of gloss, like his.
    The image seemed obscene.

She took a bath and felt the water
    Rise above her chin.
She opened up her mouth to speak
    Then, calmly, she breathed in.

Last Words at the Psychic Reading

The fortune teller's cat was born clairvoyant.
This gift for divination, slight at first,
Sharpened with age, and when Miss Lindenhurst,
Whose talent was a fraud, discovered that
The tortoiseshell could hypnotize a client,
She left the heavy lifting to the cat.

But staring down the desperate and the daft
To expedite a grift was hardly all
The cat could do. One time, on a vid-call
With a pharmacist who came back every week,
The parlor tricks gave way to real witchcraft
When feline eyes compelled the man to speak.

"My heart will stop in seven days," he said,
His voice a vulture's rasp. His body shook
Before his face resumed its normal look.
The session ended early, payment sent,
And the fortune teller scratched the cat's patched head,
Which started purring, callously content.

When a week passed, and the client did not keep
His regular appointment, Miss L knew
The omen that he'd uttered had come true.
In a dream that night, she also prophesied
The moment *she* would perish in her sleep.
The cat sat by her, watching as she died.

III

A Visit with Mrs. Pike

A Visit with Mrs. Pike

As part of her new job, Yvette drove down
To Ring's Neck, where her boss's wife,
The ailing Mrs. Pike,
Lived now, alone.
It seemed she'd come to like
To manage her husband's working life
As much as when she'd lived with him in town.

(If the law firm didn't pay Yvette so well,
And she hadn't yet been picked to lead
A major corporate case,
She might have thrown
This "meeting" in Pike's pink face—
Did someone with her skill set need
To curtsy for a sagging wife-from-hell?)

Yvette thought Pike's lake house would be immense
With gables and a turret guard,
So it surprised her when
She saw a stone-
Walled bungalow, with Zen
Or Shinto statues in the yard.
She parked on dirt; she took her phone for self-defense.

Old Mrs. Pike, who stood on a walking bridge,
Was younger by ten years at least
Than Yvette had ever guessed.
Her smooth skin shone
With health; she was simply dressed.
As she spoke, her restful forehead creased.
"You like a drink? There's fruit juice in the fridge."

Yvette was so amazed she didn't answer,
And the older woman grinned and said,
"My water garden. Yes,
It's a world of its own.
And I feel I should confess:
My husband painted me half-dead?
It's true I'm sick, but not with any cancer."

Approaching her, Yvette could see a crescent
Of sculpted pond, knee-deep, on tarp,
A languid spring-fed streaming,
A tranquil zone
Of lucid water, teeming
With big brocaded fish. "My carp.
My precious koi. So dear and iridescent,"

The young-old woman said, her voice still cheery.
"Look closer." Yvette did. She bent
At the edge, off-balance, and...
She felt her phone
Vibrating in her hand.
A text from Pike. Two words he sent:
"I'm sorry." *What the—?! This*, she thought, *is eerie.*

She dropped her phone. The koi below had changed.
The dozen or so had doubled in size,
Their bubbling water muddy.
Contorted bone
And burnished scales turned bloody.
Piranha teeth and great white eyes.
It made no sense. She had to be deranged.

The koi swam circles, snapping at the air.
A hard shove, and she toppled in.
A splash, a liquid blast.
A stifled groan.
And Mrs. Pike, at last,
Watched severed fingers float. A chin
Bobbed up. Then lips. Then hair. *Then nothing there.*

After an Industrial Accident

The Holst Mill closed for good on Christmas Eve,
And the star that led us scattered workers home
Was not a star but Saturn. Ealing Chrome
Would hire on most of us, but to believe
We felt no fear then, severance pay aside,
Was to go too far. Besides that, six had died.

The deaths came all at once, an hour before:
A crew assigned to fix a cooling bed
For I-beam steel. And now the six were dead,
Their bodies reddening the concrete floor.
Alarms—the rollers stopped—we moved to go,
Fleeing the mill to shuffle through the snow.

(The Holst Corp. footage showed an orb of white,
Like a flashbulb burst, and then its negative,
The pupil of a lidless eye. To give
A more precise report, or to say that night
What lit a cosmic flare that killed a crew,
Was more than the local fire chief could do.)

For those who chose to work in furnace heat,
Trained for smelting iron ore perhaps
Or pouring molten slag, crossing the gaps
Between the safe and the strange was no great feat.
Yet nature at its worst, we knew, could not
Produce a form so hideously wrought.

Some parts we later learned or else we dreamed.
Even the ones who'd stood outside the blast
Shunted what we'd witnessed to the past
Till visions overtook us and we screamed.
At the mill again, we watch them turned to flame
By something only exorcists could name.

Doomed Liaison

If, monstrous as I am, you should elect
To shelter me, despite the risk that I
Might yield to hunger, show my teeth, and try
Hunting you down at home, you can expect
I'll keep my distance, let you move unchecked—
*By now you're likely anxious to ask why
I'm warning you when I could sell the lie—*
Through spaces where our species intersect.

On *why*, I'm of two minds; my forebrain thinks
That for your kindness you deserve to live.
My hindbrain, now, insists that I'll regret
A bloody outcome. *So*...let's swig our drinks
And part, before I do what you *won't* forgive
And, monstrous as I am, I will forget.

The Never-Trusted Mirror

Meeting the man from outer space,
Human at least in form if not in truth,
You may well recognize his face
As one you carried in your youth

Before the Martian you became
Began to grow its onyx eyes,
And you will likely look the same
In death, to no one's great surprise.

Lines at a Wake

The first one knew the body as a baby.
She'd cradled him a quarter of his size.
A circumspect and disconcerted lady,
She couldn't trust the wisdom of her eyes.

The second mourner held a beaded rosary
Dead-gripped in her fist, a whispered prayer
Fumbled on her lips, her stance a pose she
Used to test the grief-encumbered air.

Paraded, close like cattle, past the casket,
The third an uncle, fourth a high school friend.
The fifth dropped her donation in a basket
Before she met his parents at the end.

The sixth pretended permanent confusion.
His, the most unnerving pose of all.
No one saw him enter, pale illusion
Who gaped down at his powdered face
    Like a white wax doll.

The Servant Girl

He came to fix the bathroom sink
And set his toolbox down with care—
No rattle, not a word. To think
That thin old man, his wispy hair

Still red from youth, would soon be dead,
The cause a long-expected fright,
Was nothing I'd considered. Ned—
That was his name—revealed he might

Be selling off the property:
"The manse, this carriage house, the land—
My uncle left the lot to me,
But the upkeep's gotten out of hand."

That evening when my plumbing blocked
Was his longest visit to my place,
And once he finished up, we talked
In whispers, for he seemed to trace

The source of some deep-felt unrest
To the confines of my five-room flat.
It was sad to see him so hard-pressed.
He packed his tools, and that was that

Until a few nights on he rapped
My door and joggled me from sleep.
I found him dark. His face was mapped
With lines of strain. *"I heard her weep!"*

He cried. *"She's come to take me back."*
I asked him who it was he meant.
He stood there like a maniac
Spouting froth, his tall frame bent.

I tried to take his hands and lead
Him trembling to the entryway.
He shook me off, and I could read
A mind in pain and disarray

Related through his lidless eyes.
He turned and fled. I almost ran
And caught him on the narrow rise.
Instead, I merely watched the man…

And soon an ambulance arrived.
(I don't remember dialing the phone.)
What little of his life survived
Was strapped and stretchered. Left alone,

I dressed, and waited for some sign
That Ned was dead or coming home.
He wasn't family, wasn't mine.
At once my room went monochrome.

A flickering of blue on blue
Assumed a servant's uniform,
A female face in one dull hue,
A vagrant stepping from a storm.

Her shape resolved, the blue girl glared
At me, but also far afield,
As though her sight had been impaired
When death's constrictor knot unreeled.

I forced myself to meet her gaze.
She rasped, *"He's made the sacrifice."*
Ned's spirit flashed within a maze,
And the blue girl melted out like ice.

The Dead Shape

She saw a snowy owl
And a flock of waterfowl
In a bruise-blue thunderhead,
And thought she'd rather see
The dead shape in the tree
That shadowed her bed.

Father praised her sight,
For spying in the night
The forms he called the gloom,
But Mother knew her curse,
Which merely made it worse
When sent to her room

For some too-small offense.
The dead shape was immense
And also minuscule,
A beetle and a bear,
Of a kind she couldn't share
By day at school.

She'd never heard its voice,
And if she had a choice
She wouldn't hear it now,
Yet a clicking in her ears,
A clip of pruning shears
Through a dry bough,

Or a clack of lion's teeth,
Sounded out beneath
Her pulse's heavy thud.
The dead shape said to stand.
She heeded its command
And stilled her blood.

Digging Beneath the Battlefield
Ypres, Belgium, October 1918

I

We dug; we dug for fifteen hours
With picks, pails, hauling ropes, and shovels
To twice the depth of a grave. Ours,
And by this I mean Lieutenant Lovell's
And mine, was a partnership-in-crime.
Finding China, fossils, or oil
Would've taken much less time
Than our invasion of the soil.

In the Allied Army, we'd got word
From a Belgian of a Dark One at Ypres:
A buried Worm-Chimera scored
In serpent scales and boils. The Sleeper,
Interrupted, had scorched Earth before.
We leaned to our shovels, began to dig more.

II

The chamber, when we struck its top,
Resounded like a ship's hull. We
Shuddered but didn't think to stop;
We'd brought the tools to set it free:
A welding torch, some light explosives,
A spell to lift the more arcane
Defenses. The air stank of corrosives
In the pit we'd dug. A drenching rain
Made puddles, and though it was ten days
After the battle, the mud looked red
With blood of men, or the Dark One's ichor.
We soothed our shell-shocked nerves with liquor,
Renewed our vow to join the dead
When we gave the Beast the Earth to raze.

[Note: A copy of this poem, in scrawled ink, was discovered among a war-addled private's belongings in a wing of Craiglockhart Hospital in Edinburgh at the end of 1918. The author, who died of the grippe, was from Stoke-on-Trent. There is no record of a "Lieutenant Lovell" in his battalion. An incomplete third part began simply, "We've opened Hell—such soulless eyes!" before trailing off into incoherency.]

Terzanelle for the Devil's Tour Bus

At a highway rest stop north of Providence,
My wife and I, up all night driving, slept
Slumped in our seats until the radiance

Of sunrise woke me, and I quickly swept
The sludge of slumber from my mouth and eyes.
Glancing over to see that Meg still slept,

I stretched my arms and legs. To my surprise,
A dozen yards ahead a bus was parked—
Again, I rubbed the slumber from my eyes;

It looked to me the whole of it was marked
With painted pagan symbols, bright as flame—
A dozen yards ahead a bus was parked,

Blazoned with pictographs. There was a name
Across the blackened windows: *Lord of Tours*.
Those painted pagan symbols, bright as flame—

Goat-men, serpents—leapt from yawning doors.
With Meg sleeping there north of Providence,
Our Wrangler's windshield cracked, the Lord of Tours
Revealed to me his hellish radiance.

The Wrong Stop

I fell asleep while on the bus;
   Forgot to pull the cord.
The driver I named Gloomy Gus
   Pressed onward as I snored.

I woke up with a jolt, and I
   Could tell the time was wrong.
The afternoon had left the sky—
   The lunar light was strong.

Across, another rider, tall
   And skeletally thin,
Was whistling with a dying fall,
   But I cannot begin

To say—I'd lost all sense of place—
   Where I had seen his kind
Or how his wasted wax-doll face
   Had meddled with my mind.

His piping paused; he didn't speak,
   So I could hear a bell
Colliding with the engine's shriek
   As Gus called, *"Next stop—Hell."*

I turned. My window showed a field
   Of devastated grain;
Its locust-ridden rows appealed
   To the sick parts of my brain.

Then a borderland where biting flies
   The size of great horned owls
Patrolled the close, necrotic skies.
   That's when I caught the howls

From cauldrons boiling naked damned
   That followed on our tour.
I shot up, reached the back, and slammed,
   In panic, on the door.

"I'm dreaming! No! It's just a dream!"
   I hollered myself hoarse.
I crumpled, wept. I couldn't scream,
   So Gus obliged, of course.

IV

The Horror Artist

The Horror Artist

She draws the damned in chalk pastels,
Blending the bright hues on black.
This gives a luster to the hells
She draws. The damned in chalk pastels
All gleam like lanternfish. She tells
Herself she's doomed to be a hack.
She draws the damned in chalk pastels,
Blending the bright hues on black.

Her face is always there among
The tortured souls in cover sketches.
She's shrieking, swallowing her tongue.
Her face is always there. Among
The scraps she's kept since she was young
Is one where she's the queen of wretches.
Her face, it's always there among
The tortured souls in cover sketches.

The Graves

I

When Conlan stepped within the square of stones,
Red leaves were tumbling in a sudden gust;
And the town's surveyor, trembling, thought there must
Be something to these do-not-enter zones.
His contract said to set up safety cones
And yellow tape around the land in trust;
But once inside he found that he could just
Stand dazed and close-to-blind in cold unknowns.

The map they gave him named the rock-walled site
As a former farmer's plat, or a cow's ground,
Yet grass alone now grew there, scarred with blight
As though crop circles compassed each stone mound
That marked a burial plot—the chill air bright
And loud (*so loud*)—or was it his pulse's pound?

II

Patrolman Wedge saw Conlan's empty car
Off-road at dawn, his quiet night shift done,
But didn't run the plates. In the fall sun
He knew at once who owned the Ford. At a bar
He liked, he'd met the guy—a football star
At Hollis High some years before—and none
Of his bells rang; he never touched his gun;
And yet the setting struck him as bizarre.

Wedge moved to search the car, then heard a crack
From in the yard. He called out to a wraith,
With no response. A queer thing held him back:
Where seven mounds were, now there was an eighth.
A white stone thrust from gummy earth, in truth,
The way his baby daughter cut a tooth.

Your Sunday Shirt

I leave your laundry swaying
On the line behind the shack,
With our bloodhound outside baying,
But I'm not looking back
At the red splotch on the shoulder
    Of your Sunday shirt;
That stain has started to molder,
    And isn't dirt.

I might have let it burn up
In the wood stove as I did
Your meal of beef and turnip,
And the stray red hairs you hid,
From the slain girl, in the curtain
    Beside our bed,
But I wanted to be certain
    I've hanged what's dead.

And I could have called a neighbor
Or left you to police,
Yet *I* took on the labor
When you said she was your niece,
And you said it close to proudly,
    And I was your wife,
And you said it again, more loudly—
    So I used a knife.

Gods of the Garden

Gods of the garden are growing thin,
And no one knows how long this night
Or nightmare may emaciate them further.
Dawn, in truth, was due eleven days ago,
But who has seen the sun, our sleeping star?
The first to feel night's scythe was Feverfew,
The deity of daisies, then Daffodil,
Whose yellow bulbs have blanched,
Her flower-faces furred with fungus now.
Roots are more resilient, and the steady rain
Is soaking succor for them. Still,
To live they must have light, or all is leaf-fall
And petal-plummeting. We pray for morning,
Hoping against hope doomed Hollyhocks will heal.

Loyal Companion

Being a dog of war, a trench-bred cur,
I wake in mud beside my sleeping master
And snap at a rat that crept too close to camp.
The rat is fast, but I am faster.

Then, having breakfasted, I prop my head
Against my master's rifle barrel. Dawn
Gnaws hard at the black bones of night,
And as it breaks, I growl, *Sleep on.*

An hour. And now the company has stirred.
Twelve men, two dogs. I nip my master's shin,
Expecting him to flinch and quickly rouse,
But he's gone stiff, his heart done in.

I wait till someone comes, but who is this?
The stinks of muck and ash confuse my nose.
My master's shape it is, but not his face.
This face is pearly, and it glows.

Being a dog of war, a soldier's mongrel,
I leap up at his call, his voice a boy's,
And leave my filthy bed, my fur, to chase
Him out of smoke and out of noise.

The Mixed Marriage

I

The men grew tired of the candle-lighter's stares
And sent her grumbling from the judgment room
To speak unhindered of the bride and groom
Whose marriage they'd rejected. *"Damned if there's
Not treason in this, to catch us unawares
Like beardless novices,"* said Elder Bloom.
"The Parson's done it." Silent in the gloom,
The other Elders shifted in their chairs,
Five men with Bloom presiding over court.
"The Parson knows his duty to the Law,"
Said Elder Root. *"I scarce think he's the sort
To desecrate our Church with such a flaw
As amounts to grievous sin. It's nothing short
Of sacrilege to join up Hand with Claw."*

II

Not far away, those very newlyweds—
A Village man and an Owlish woman—slept
In an earthy cellar-space where farmers kept
Their winter stores in jars. Few marriage beds
Were harder, sure, but through the lovers' heads
A common dream of perfect comfort swept.
They could have dozed for hours there, except
The sack they used for cover tore to shreds
As they woke in fright to a stomping up above.
The man, whose name was Branch, held in a breath
And clutched his finely feathered wife, his Grace.
"If the Elders come, I'll hold them off, my love."
The open cellar door meant certain death,
Yet in the light was the kindly Parson's face.

III

That night they found the Parson in the wood.
He was alone and praying on his knees,
His voice and arms uplifted to the trees.
The Elders, nearing, quickly understood
The pair was gone, and it would do no good
To track them in the wild. The Parson's pleas
Rang hollow now; the only guarantees
Were a rope, a gallows, and a hangman's hood.
The Elders had brought torches, and their glow
Caught silhouettes of raptors on the boughs:
Six-foot falcons fixed like heavy snow,
A wingéd woman, beaked, with Owlish brows
Leering at the huddled men below,
Leaping down to keep her wedding vows.

A Shiver on the Crosstown Bus

Garlic Enthusiast Found Dead
appeared as breaking news, and Beth,
amused despite the mention of death,
smirked at her phone and shook her head.
The joke was in how the first two words
did not connect with what came next,
two chunked-together lumps of text
like *Cotton Candy Mangles Birds*.
She skimmed the story, scrolling down
past ads for shoes, and learned the late
H. Mervin Schloss, aged eighty-eight,
was found, throat cut, just north of town.
Beth gulped at that; her scrolling slowed,
the humor in the headline gone.
Police said hunters stumbled on
the corpse in a culvert off the road.
The coroner had much to share
about the wounds, the lack of blood,
how Schloss's body, caked in mud,
had garlic cloves in clothes and hair.
Bizarre, Beth thought. She rushed to read
the rest before her stop. No more;
the screen went blank. She loudly swore,
but no one paid her any heed.
She didn't care. She jerked her phone,
a jolt to bring it back to life.
News Flash: Leech Farmer Murders Wife.
She fled the bus, raced home alone.

This Borrowed Thing

When Henley saw her mother's wedding dress,
She said, flat out, "I'd rather wear a bag."
Her maid of honor, Jill, whose suggestion it was
To revive Hen's late mom's boxed-up gown, regretted
Recommending it. But her friend had fretted
For weeks in bridal shops, forlorn because
Perfection added thousands to the tag
And Hen had debts, her father's life a mess.

With two months until the nuptials, Henley caved,
And they found a seamstress to make alterations.
The long train had to go; nothing was clearer.
At the fitting, Hen looked beautiful, Jill thought.
This borrowed thing was better than something bought.
Still, Hen broke out in hives as she stood at the mirror:
"The dress is shit, and we've sent the invitations."
Jill tried to soothe her, but the moment couldn't be saved.

(The two had not discussed Hen's mother's death.
It happened the last year they were both at school.
The obit said "illness," but Jill knew suicide
Was the end result no matter how it started.
When she met Billy, Hen seemed brokenhearted,
Drifting from job to job. To be a bride
Became her only goal. "I'd be a fool,"
She said, "to turn down bells and baby's breath.")

A second round of fixes, and the gown
Was ready. This boosted Henley's confidence
And Jill's resolve to see the wedding through,
Dress or no dress, to its proper conclusion,
And all went as she hoped, without confusion
Or frigid feet. They had nothing left to do
The night before but sleep; it made good sense
To turn in early, so they soon lay down

In hotel beds in adjoining rooms. Hen dreamed
Of flowers in bouquets, while Jill woke trembling,
Too thrown to click her bedside lamp. She peered
Into the dark as a streak of white emerged
Out of the wall, a gauzy form that surged
To the end of her bed and took the shape she feared:
A woman, veiled, in a long-trained dress resembling
One drowned. At the figure's bloody wrists Jill screamed.

The Butter Knife

The butter knife was blunted at both ends,
And none would say it ever left the table,
Least of all the countess and her friends.
Her chair had four thick legs yet felt unstable.

While none would say it ever left the table,
The butter knife, the countess thought, depends
(Her chair had four thick legs yet felt unstable)
For placement on how far its blade extends.

The butter knife, the countess thought, depends
(What made her think at once of Cain and Abel?)
For balance on how much its handle bends,
Its steel as strong, its trim as taut as cable.

What made her think at once of Cain and Abel?
The count sat like a mooning boy who spends
(Its blunted edge, its old Parisian label)
His fortunes on a mob of make-pretends.

The count sat like a mooning boy who spends
His days apart, no one to join his fable,
His fortunes not enough to make amends,
As the countess donned a veil, a gown of sable.

She dined alone, no husband at her table—
The bitter knife now bloodied at both ends—
And the women walked to church in gowns of sable,
That beastly dowager countess and her friends.

Meerwich Library

Meerwich Library has a lowest level
Where stairs and elevators do not go.
The superstitious might suppose a devil
Had dug its lair there, but the keepers know
No purpose for that story. The architects,
Dross, Mountebank & Mori, had fixed a trap
In the upper floor that, edgewise, intersects,
When opened, with the building's deepest gap
Accessible by rope or by a lunge
Into a black that lamplight can't expunge.

For ninety years, the sharpest intellects
From Angstrom University have tried to map
Wellsprings of that space, and their work rejects
The "wormhole postulation" held by Rapp
And Thornton. Here's a counterquote from Neville:
"Our instruments and observations show
The Meerwich Athenaeum's lowest level—
Impervious to any shine or glow,
Repellent as a kleptolucent sponge—
Is bottomless, and nowhere we should plunge."

V

A Means of Summoning

A Means of Summoning
For M.R. James

Wry spirit, sessile as a pondweed, wake.
Sleep does not become you, nor the ebb
Of water through a water spider's web,
So large the diving bell could catch a snake
Where striders cross the wobble of the lake
To end life in a mallard's yellow nib,
The opposite of Eve from Adam's rib,
For any sense these correlations make.

In "A Warning to the Curious" you'll note
One squat martello tower on a bluff
(As troublous now as was it when you wrote)
Is, in its way, analogous enough
To how your soul has settled to rebuff
The notion that Old Scratch should hold your coat.

Unrest Settlement, Dakota Territory

We'd both been looking outward at the hills
That formed the northern border of the Square
When I said to Mama, "Death won't come from there."
She nodded, adding, "Sleep's the thing that kills."
With a tremor she'd got from working in the mills
Twelve years in Stowe, she knelt as if in prayer:
"And you, your daddy's son, know Sleep is where
You must not go. We slumber as God wills."

I almost said that God had fled Unrest
And left the last of us to stagger on,
But, sure she would have cuffed my cheek, I lied:
"The Lord is good. Amen." I thought it best
To leave her be. I stretched and stifled a yawn,
Knew thirty hours had passed since Daddy died

      And Mama alone had cried.
(There were no other mourners in that place.)
Though I didn't weep, I showed upon my face
      A halfway Christian grace.
When Sleep took Mama, I was too tired for rites.
I aimed for the hills—still hope to tread their heights.

The Mad Monologue of Doctor Chronology

Any heart this world possesses must be dead.
And no, no other worlds exist. You're free
To scoff, but I insist—Infinity
Hangs bleak and wholly heartless. I have said
As much to colleagues who would comprehend
The horrifying costs of cheating Time,
That knowing every outcome, every end
Before its cause, is tantamount to...*I'm
Afraid you'll have to nurse the glass I poured...*
Is tantamount to rigging every game
Of take-your-chance and reaping no reward.
Yes, yes—I could reveal to you his name
And home address. However, you should think—
Here, I'll buy us both another drink—
No matter what the bastard's done to you,
What good would any retribution do?
Let's say, by day, he manages a store,
An unassuming alter ego for
A savior from a distant crimson sun.
You storm into his workplace with a gun,
Rejoicing in each bloody trigger-pull.
(*I see your eyes; you'd down a barrelful.*)
Then let's suppose he's quick enough to palm
Or misdirect your bullets. Do you bomb
A bus (no muss, no fuss) on second try,
While hiding in some rat-infested lair,
And feel him fall, a comet from the sky,
To cage you with his subatomic stare?
My boy, I have stood by and watched you fail,
Your machinations come to no avail,
For it's the nature of my power to cast
My aura to the future or the past.
Go home—*don't be like me*—I've lost the art.
Tomorrow, find yourself a steady job—
I hear they're hiring muscle for the mob—
Or disbelieve, and dog your own dead heart.

The Hunting Party

The hunting party found the body first,
A woman half-immersed
In sluggish river, half in mud.
The dogs had run, attracted by the blood,
And the four old hunters, hoping for a deer,
Saw a human face where the water washed it clear.

"No more than a girl," the oldest among them said.
Her tangled hair was red,
And she looked more like a debutante,
Dead in a muddy dress, than someone's aunt,
The youngest thought. The other two kept back
And leashed the dogs, still barking as a pack.

A single call would bring the state police,
If they had a phone. (There's peace
In going off the grid, they knew.)
Two men said they would stay behind; the two
With dogs would hike the woods to a nearby road.
The body waited, and the river slowed.

"If this is murder," one began. He scanned
The riverbanks, his hand
Tapping the barrel of his gun.
The other knelt and smoked. The morning sun
Played tricks with colors, painting her white face
Blue-black, as though she were another race.

"It is," the kneeler said, noting the gash
Across her throat. The ash
Fell from his cigarette; the smoke
Concealed the smell of rot. The younger spoke
Of crime-scene tape, of leaving the body be.
His friend stayed put. "Death's close enough for me."

The Burning Man

The burning man is after me;
He ate the forest, tree by tree.
He's slim of limb and thin of skin.
He rings the flaming orchard in
His arms of Agent Orange, and
A swarm of aphids in his hand.

The burning man has eaten well,
And by his leavings I can tell
He favors cherry over pear;
He flings the pits, a browsing bear;
But even though he's sated, he
Will clear another plate for me.

The burning man is instant blight:
An ash-black thumb, a torch to light
The stubble fields in Stygian mist
Like kindling for an arsonist.
I can't deter him, nor assuage;
He hunts for pleasure, not for rage.

The burning man is growing wise
To where I run. His mantis eyes
Are now protruding to the sea—
Too soon he will be done with me—
Up the headland, down the pier:
His wicker crown is here, is here!

What Sank in Magpie Lake

What sank in Magpie Lake did not return,
As we who lived beside it were to learn
Last August and the dreadful months that followed
When a wading mother watched her daughter drown—
The water grew a mouth, she said, and swallowed—
Before the county closed the beaches down.

Three swimmers died last year, the girl, two men,
Though none of them was ever seen again,
And some who lived beside the lapping water
But would not move away avoid it still—
I ought to know; that devil took my daughter—
Certain it will never eat its fill.

The Death of the Sculptor's Model

In a bleak mood, the morning of her wake,
The sculptor took a hammer to the bust
Made in her likeness. Blind to his mistake
And bludgeoning the desolated base,
He stomped the shattered plaster into dust
Like powder they had painted on her face.

To pay for Christian burial, he'd sold
Off all his lover's other effigies.
She was, he shuddered, seventeen years old
When fever left her raving in their bed
While he recovered from the same disease—
And he was fifty. She alone was dead.

Kneeling now, he held the hammer up;
He figured he could swing it hard enough
To pulverize his skull like a china cup
Or an eggshell. He wanted so to chase her.
She had no way he knew to call his bluff,
And so he struck, the sooner to embrace her.

The Closed Casket

Years back, to pay for school, I spent my summers
Driving a hearse for Daggett & Macduff,
Which remains the nicest funeral home in town.
Dressed in a suit, I shuttled the dear departed
To their gravesites, often leading a slow procession
Like the boatman on the River Styx. (Or not—
I've taught the Greeks so long I'm apt to change
The worldly to the mythic. But I'm stalling.)
The morning when I lifted the coffin lid,
I'd come in early to help out Mr. Daggett,
Arranging chairs and three-foot wreaths of flowers
For a large and pricey service. "A sad one, this,"
The director said as he placed a woman's photo
On a music stand beside the closed-topped casket.
"Kelsey Niles. Just thirty. Apartment fire."
The raw facts startled me, yet it was her face,
Pretty but drained—a single mom?—half-smiling,
Green eyes, a fringe of blonde, that made me stare.
"Came over from the coroner's. Her son..."
He swallowed, stayed composed. "...was badly burned.
Still, though, they say he'll live, poor boy. Yes, sad."
I nodded. Mr. D did not speak much,
But prepping for the wake had made him chatty.
His smartphone hummed, and he left to take the call
Outside the viewing room. Abandoned now
With Kelsey Niles, her body boxed, I flinched
And stepped away. I'd never been alone
With someone dead before. I'd always had
At least one stressed mortician, a mob of mourners
Surrounding me. The bodies then were objects,
Were empty weights for me to move on wheels—
Important, sure, like precious pieces of luggage,
But not at all like *this* here now. What lay
Inside the casket once had breathed, had smiled,
Had loved her son. I suddenly needed to see.

I approached the box and, raising the lid, I saw
Something I can't forget, that jars me still.
This wasn't your standard stiff in a burial dress;
She was a sleeping queen from a country of spiders.
A thin shroud covered her frame from head to toe.
In the white web her shape was girlish, unclothed.
The fire had charred the skin of her arms and chest.
Her face was spared, eyes shut, and as I looked,
The shroud began to smolder in smokeless flames.
The body jolted. Dead eyes opened wide,
And dead mouth whispered *Jamie* to her son.
Dead hands reached up for me. I slammed the lid
And ran from the room, colliding with Mr. D,
Who, seeing my speechless fear, would let me go
Without a question, knowing as I did
That day was my last at Daggett & Macduff.

To Gaelle Lacroix, Lone Survivor
of the Trufort Massacre

You leave me sad and sleepless, and your story,
As much a folktale as a horror yarn,
A carnival of shades and sordid shames
From small Maine towns with long Acadian names,
Began at birth and ended with that gory
Sanguination in a storm-scarred barn.

You lost your mother and older sister then.
Your father, a long-haul trucker, was away
In a motel outside New York City when
The bloodshed started that November day,
A week before you made it, Gaelle, to five.
What kept you, after all you saw, alive?

The local paper branded it "mass murder"
And called your mother's group a "Christian cult,"
Its leader, Jensen Carr, a "roving preacher"
And army vet from Kennebec. Consult
The next day's news: *Daughter Of Preschool Teacher
Hides In Box Through Slayings; No One Heard Her—*

"Her" being *you*, of course—you stayed so silent
While Shepherd Carr and his "gun dogs" turned violent,
Shooting sixteen followers and, later,
Themselves, with Carr convinced there was a traitor
In his fold. But all (save you) were dead, and free
From needing to confess to treachery.

About those deaths, here's what you do not know:
Carr's target was a church in Orono
That had a lesbian woman as its pastor,
But when he sensed a snitch, the shepherd snapped
And, as you must recall, it all moved faster
Than anyone foresaw. It left you trapped

And shaking in an empty moving box.
Did your mother stash you there, or did you climb
Inside on instinct when the first shots sounded?
At four years old, did your sweetened sense of time
Go sour in you, like grapes to the fabled fox,
Or could you hear the cops had the barn surrounded?

Soon after, social services stepped in
And drove you to a safe house for the night
Where, hopefully, you slept, and slept, and woke
Only when your father came and spoke
To you in his most gentle voice. There might
Have been wolf-whiskers growing from his chin,

And you were in your crimson riding hood,
For you'd become at once a changeling child
That goblins gifted to a wifeless man.
How long until he drops you in the wood,
Abandons you to creatures of the wild?
You'd better run, as quickly as you can.

I'm pondering your French surname—*the cross*.
You're much too young to have its weight to bear.
The world has spared you, yet it fails to care.
I leave you to your nightmare and your loss.
I pray there'll be a lucky lightning-flash
To burn that old barn down to smoke and ash.

Feeding the Chickens

They know when the girl has been to school.
The sweat of other children blurs
        With her own sweet scent. But as a rule,
Only the broody hens let show the ache
        The whole flock feels. Combined with hers
Is the stink of hawk and snake.

Late afternoon the girl brings in
The pails: alfalfa meal, field peas,
        And corn. The purple bruise on her chin
Is a gift from Papa. The brute, he took the eggs
        Two hours ago and went. Her knees
Are scabbed; her arms, her legs.

No hen will fly the coop; they're bred
For laying, not for choosing sides—
        Buff Orpington, Rhode Island Red—
Yet still, each simple brain goes humanly dark,
        Grows geniuslike, till each one hides
A vengeful undermark.

The girl who feeds them does not see
This inner turn; these ladies appear
        As biddable as ever. She
Cuddles them; they fluff their tails. A mouse
        Runs past. She follows, does not fear
What leaps toward Papa's house.

Acknowledgments of Prior Publications

Many poems in this collection were first published in the author's self-published chapbooks, *The Sun Ships* (2019) and *The Bedlam Philharmonic* (2020), as well as his collaborative collection with Frank Coffman, *The Exorcised Lyric* (2021), from Mind's Eye Publications.

Some also appear in following journals or anthologies:

Dreams & Nightmares
"The Mad Monologue of Doctor Chronology"

Epitaphs: The Journal of the New England Horror Writers
"Lines at a Wake"

Penumbra
"Scabrous Oak"

Space and Time
"The Nothing Box"

Spectral Realms
"Caged Animals"; "The Burning Man"; "A Means of Summoning"; "What Came of the Search"; "Digging Beneath the Battlefield"; "Ghosts in Their Sunday Clothes"; "Loyal Companion"; "After an Industrial Accident"; "The Death of the Sculptor's Model"; "Gods of the Garden"; "The Bedlam Philharmonic"; "The Graves"; and "To Gaelle Lacroix, Lone Survivor of the Trufort Massacre"

The Vampiricon: Imaginings & Images of the Vampire
"Doomed Liaison"

Notes on Forms

I. Caged Animals
"Caged Animals" is in a nonce form.
"Ghosts in Their Sunday Clothes" is a villanelle.
"The Scourge of Song" is a ballade.
"Designer Ghosts" is an English sonnet.
"The Druggist's Curse" is a pair of Italian sonnets.
"What Came of the Search" is in a nonce form.
"The Bedlam Philharmonic" is in a nonce form.
"The Interlopers" has a warped-mirrored rhyme scheme.
"Second Sight" is in a nonce form.
"The Nothing Box" is a 15-line sonnet.

II.   The Cruel Become Werewolves
"The Cruel Become Werewolves" is in a nonce form.
"Glenwell's Son" is in heroic couplets.
"A Blue Giraffe" is in varied tetrameter dizains.
"Scabrous Oak" is in tetrameter quatrains.
"The Flower-Faced Boy at the Mall" is an Italian sonnet.
"The Gray Kid" is in sonnets.
"Rats" is in a nonce form.
"When Mother Taught Me Hymns" is in long measure.
"The Green-Eyed Man" is in ballad stanzas.
"Last Words at the Psychic Reading" is in a nonce form.

III.   A Visit with Mrs. Pike
"A Visit with Mrs Pike" is in a nonce form.
"After an Industrial Accident" is in heroic sestets.
"Doomed Liaison" is an Italian sonnet.
"The Never-Trusted Mirror" is in tetrameter quatrains.
"Lines at a Wake" is in a nonce form.
"The Servant Girl" is in cross-rhyming tetrameter quatrains.
"The Dead Shape" is in a nonce form.
"Digging Beneath the Battlefield" is in four-beat English sonnets.
"Terzanelle for the Devil's Tour Bus" is a terza rima villanelle.
"The Wrong Stop" is in ballad meter.

IV. The Horror Artist

"The Horror Artist" is in a nonce form.
"The Graves" is a pair of Italian sonnets.
"Your Sunday Shirt" is in a nonce form.
"Gods of the Garden" is based on strong-stress alliterative meter.
"Loyal Companion" is in a nonce form.
The Mixed Marriage" is in Italian sonnets.
"A Shiver on the Crosstown Bus" is in a nonce form.
"This Borrowed Thing" has a reflexive rhyme scheme.
"The Butter Knife" is a pantoum.
"Meerwich Library" is a variation on the English sonnet.

V. A Means of Summoning

"A Means of Summoning" is a variation on the Italian sonnet.
"Unrest Settlement, Dakota Territory" is a caudate sonnet.
"The Mad Monologue of Doctor Chronology" is in a nonce form.
"The Hunting Party" is in a nonce form.
"The Burning Man" is in a nonce form.
"What Sank in Magpie Lake" is in a nonce form.
"The Death of the Sculptor's Model" is in a nonce form.
"The Closed Casket" is in blank verse.
"To Gaelle Lacroix" is in heroic sestets.
"Feeding the Chickens" is in a nonce form.